A catalogue record for this book is available
from the British Library

Published by Ladybird Books Ltd
A subsidiary of the Penguin Group
A Pearson Company
© LADYBIRD BOOKS LTD MCMXCVII

LADYBIRD and the device of a Ladybird are trademarks of
Ladybird Books Ltd Loughborough Leicestershire UK

# SPELLING
### AND
# GRAMMAR

*by* Audrey Daly
*illustrated by* David Till

# CONTENTS

## INTRODUCTION

Everyone wants to be able to write good English, because it is useful in so many ways. Whether you're writing a letter to your mother, writing a play to put on with friends, or just filling in an application form for a competition, it helps to understand how our language works.

To write well, you need a sound knowledge of sentence structure, punctuation and spelling. There are rules to help you, to show you how to avoid common mistakes.

And the more you study each one and put it into practice, the easier it will become, until in the end you will be able to write good English without thinking about it.

IT'S EASY

ENGLISH GRAMMAR
SPELLING
VOCABULARY
TENSES
PUNCTUATION
ADJECTIVES
VERBS
NOUNS

# THE USE OF ENGLISH

English is an international language, spoken by 1500 million people – more than a quarter of the entire population of the Earth. It is also the language of science and technology, used by people of different nations to communicate new ideas and discoveries. Its present form has developed from a number of ancient languages, enriched year by year, century by century, from many sources. It is a flexible language with a huge vocabulary.

Written English uses the **Roman alphabet**, which has 26 letters altogether. Five of these are vowels – a e i o u – and 21 are consonants – b c d f g h j k l m n p q r s t v w x y z.

The order of the alphabet is used letter by letter to sort lists and information of all kinds, making it easy to find.

Libraries, reference books, telephone directories and computers all use alphabetical order, and so do UK postcodes and the British car registration system.

The alphabet is also used to make up the words we write in English. Nearly all words have vowels in them, and some – such as **facetious** and **tambourine** – contain all five. Words without vowels usually have the letter y in them, used as a vowel – **hymn** and **why** are among these.

To learn the meaning and spelling of new words, use a dictionary. To learn new phrases and ways to express what you want to say, use a thesaurus.

Where's my number plate?

POLICE

# BUILDING A SENTENCE

A **sentence** is a group of words starting with a capital letter and ending with a full stop, question mark or exclamation mark. It almost always has a verb, which is the action or 'doing' word. These are all sentences:

I eat a sandwich.

Where is your cat?

Stop that!

I don't believe it!

A sentence also has a **subject**. The person or thing doing the action is the subject. This can be either a noun or a pronoun – that is, a word used in place of a noun.

If the subject is doing something to someone or something, that someone or something becomes the **object** of the sentence. This too can be either a noun or a pronoun.

The girl climbed a tree.
subject   verb   object

If you want to say more about the girl or the tree, you can add an **adjective**.

The young girl climbed a tall tree.

The adjective 'young' tells you what the girl was like.
The adjective 'tall' tells you what the tree was like.

If you want to say more about how she climbed the tree, you can use an **adverb**.

The young girl quickly climbed a tall tree.

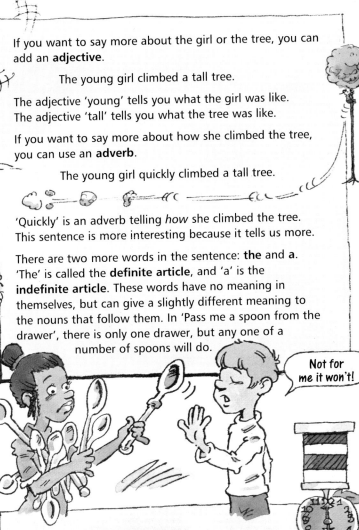

'Quickly' is an adverb telling *how* she climbed the tree.
This sentence is more interesting because it tells us more.

There are two more words in the sentence: **the** and **a**.
'The' is called the **definite article**, and 'a' is the **indefinite article**. These words have no meaning in themselves, but can give a slightly different meaning to the nouns that follow them. In 'Pass me a spoon from the drawer', there is only one drawer, but any one of a number of spoons will do.

Not for me it won't!

**An** is another form of 'a', used in front of a noun starting with a vowel – eg an apple. It is also used in front of words starting with a silent 'h' – an hour, an honour.

11

# MORE ABOUT SENTENCES

Sentences are built up with nine main different **parts of speech**:

| | |
|---|---|
| Noun | names things or people |
| Pronoun | used instead of a noun to avoid repetition |
| Verb | action or doing word |
| Adjective | describes things or people |
| Adverb | alters the meaning of the verb slightly |
| Preposition | relates one thing to another |
| Conjunction | joins words or sentences together |
| Interjection | a short word showing emotion or feeling |
| Articles | a, an – indefinite articles |
| | the – definite article |

"Hooray!" shouted Cilla, as she leapt gracefully over the tall hurdle.

| | |
|---|---|
| "Hooray!" | *interjection* |
| shouted | *verb* |
| Cilla, | *proper noun (subject)* |
| as | *conjunction* |
| she | *pronoun* |
| leapt | *verb* |
| gracefully | *adverb* |
| over | *preposition* |
| the | *article* |
| tall | *adjective* |
| hurdle. | *noun* |

## TYPES OF SENTENCES

A **simple** sentence describes only one thing or idea, and has only one verb.

The headteacher sometimes rides a horse.
My mother likes dogs.
Kevin's father has a new car.

**Complex** sentences describe more than one thing or idea, and have more than one verb in them.

iaow!

The headteacher sometimes rides a horse that belongs to her brother.
My mother likes dogs that don't bark.
Kevin's father has a new car that goes fast.

Sometimes you can turn complex sentences into simple sentences:

The headteacher sometimes rides her brother's horse.
Kevin's father has a new fast car.

**Compound** sentences are made up of two or more simple sentences combined by using conjunctions.

The sun was setting in the west, and the moon was just rising.

# NOUNS

Everything and every person has a name, and that name is a **noun**.

**Common nouns** describe general things or people. All these are common nouns:

book

car

boy

police

furniture

buildings

food

**Proper nouns** always start with a capital letter. Your own name is a proper noun. So are the names of your friends.

I'm on my way!

David   Ahmed   Jessica   Rosemary   Kevin are all proper nouns.

The names of places are proper nouns as well:
London
New York
Africa
Japan
America

Official titles are also proper nouns:

President Clinton
Pope John Paul II
Queen Elizabeth II
Prime Minister of Australia

**Abstract nouns** are the names given to emotions or ideas:

joy

wisdom

hope

honesty

anger

crime

Nouns can also tell you the **gender** – whether the word is male, female or neuter (that is, without sex). Words which are common gender can be either masculine or feminine.

| *Masculine* | *Feminine* | *Neuter* | *Common gender* |
|---|---|---|---|
| monk | nun | lamp | swimmer |
| father | mother | cupboard | owner |
| gander | goose | van | driver |
| nephew | niece | wind | player |

15

# MORE ABOUT NOUNS

A **singular noun** is just one thing:

| | |
|---|---|
| a smile | an egg |
| the match | one finger |

To make a singular noun into a **plural noun** (more than one thing), add **-s** or **-es**.

| | |
|---|---|
| smiles | eggs |
| matches | fingers |

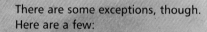

There are some exceptions, though. Here are a few:

| | | | |
|---|---|---|---|
| foot | feet | man | men |
| child | children | woman | women |
| tooth | teeth | knife | knives |

**Collective nouns** (sometimes known as **group terms**) are the names of whole groups. They can be the names of living groups:

More like a forest!

a litter of kittens
a school of porpoises
a basketball team
a troop of monkeys
a crowd of people

Non-living things also have collective nouns to describe them:

How about a friendly game?

a fleet of aircraft carriers
a library of books
a pack of cards

Collective nouns are usually singular, and have no capital letters:

The herd of cows is stampeding towards me.

A herd of bulls, you mean.

# PRONOUNS

When you want your sentences to flow more smoothly, avoiding clumsy repetition, you use **pronouns** in place of nouns. Here are two ways of saying the same thing:

a) Susie went to sleep. Susie dreamed about the circus.
b) Susie went to sleep. She dreamed about the circus.

In b), the pronoun 'she' is used to avoid repeating the noun 'Susie'. It's important to make clear what or whom the pronoun refers to.

**Personal pronouns** used as the **subject** of a sentence are:

| I | you | he | she | it | we | they |
|---|-----|-----|------|----|-----|------|

**I** looked at Jeremy.
**He** fed the baby.

Personal pronouns can also be used as the **object** of a sentence. Here are some examples:

| me | you | him | her | it | us | them |
|----|-----|-----|-----|----|-----|------|

I looked at **him**.
He fed **her**.

18

Sometimes personal pronouns are turned into **compound pronouns** by adding 'self' or 'selves'. This is in sentences where the subject and object are the same person or people. Compound pronouns are:

Himself

Myself

Itself

Herself

Themselves

Yourself

Ourselves

| myself | yourself | himself | herself | itself |
|--------|----------|---------|---------|--------|
| ourselves | yourselves | themselves | | |

The baby can feed **herself** now.
They like to have the house to **themselves**.

**Possessive pronouns** are used in place of nouns that show possession. Such nouns always have an apostrophe, for example Damien's. These are the possessive pronouns:

| mine | yours |
|------|-------|
| his | hers |
| its | ours |
| yours | theirs |

Is that book Jessica's?

No, it is mine. Hers is on the table.

19

# ADJECTIVES

**Adjectives** are describing words that give additional information about a noun or pronoun.

The **huge** castle had **strong** walls and **round** turrets.

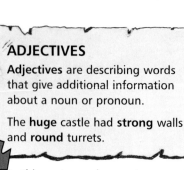

In this sentence, huge, strong and round are all adjectives.

The main or **simple** form of an adjective is that given in a dictionary:

fast   brave   kind

To compare two things or persons, we use **comparative adjectives**, and for most of these, just add **r** or **er** to the simple form:

faster   braver   kinder

Sometimes spelling changes must be made to longer adjectives before adding **er**:

YAH BOO   OH YEAH?

ugly   uglier

change y to i, +er

heavy   heavier

The comparative can also be shown by adding **more** in front of the simple form:

more merciful      more cheerful

**+MORE**

When comparing three or more things or people, **superlative adjectives** are used. Most of these are formed by adding **st** or **est** to the simple adjective:

**+st or +est**

fast fastest    brave bravest    kind kindest

Longer adjectives often use **most** in front of the simple form to produce the superlative:

LEAVE TOWN

YOU ARE MOST MERCIFUL!

YOU'VE MADE ME THE MOST CHEERFUL GIRL!

**MOST**

**most** merciful      **most** cheerful

HE'S THE MOST!

Some of the commonest adjectives follow none of these rules:

| Adjective | Comparative | Superlative |
|-----------|-------------|-------------|
| little | less | least |
| many | more | most |
| good | better | best |
| bad | worse | worst |

## MORE ABOUT ADJECTIVES

**Adjectives of quantity** show how much or how many of
the noun is being talked about. Here are some examples:

> all   both   many   some   several   double

> There were several people in the room.
> I have many friends.

Numbers are also used as adjectives of quantity:

> two cakes and five buns
> the first computer
> my third sandwich

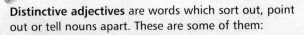

**Distinctive adjectives** are words which sort out, point out or tell nouns apart. These are some of them:

    this   every   each   neither   which

Some distinctive adjectives ask questions about the noun or pronoun, such as:

Which?

What?

Whose?

Whose coat is this?

Distinctive adjectives also point out which noun or pronoun is being talked about, such as:
this   that   these   those

That coat is Jane's.

Finding just the right adjective can be fun. Careful and varied use of adjectives can help to make your writing vivid and lively.

# VERBS

HELP!

Almost every sentence needs a **verb**. Verbs are very important words, both in speech and writing. They are called 'doing' words, because they show what is happening. Here are some examples:

speak   drive   climb   run   play

My mother drives a van.
Jenny climbs trees.
His cousin plays the recorder.

Other verbs show the way something is, such as:

am   is   are

The players are on the football pitch.
The chimpanzee is in the grass.
I am happy.

## AUXILIARY VERBS

Two or more words are needed from time to time to make up a verb, and these are called **auxiliary** (or helping) **verbs**.

Here is a list of auxiliary verbs:

had   have   has   can   could   do   did
is   are   am   was   were   may   might
should   would   will   shall

She could never find her keys.
He can play tennis quite well.
Dad will be going to the match.

VOTE FOR ME

24

## NOUN/VERB AGREEMENT

The subject of a verb can be either one person or thing (**singular**) or more than one (**plural**).

When the subject is singular, the verb must also be singular, and with a plural subject, the verb must be plural.

singular   I cook, you cook, he, she, or it cooks
plural     we cook,   you cook,   they cook

**Here, chickie.**

He cooks casseroles in the oven.
They cook chicken on the barbecue.

When a verb ends in **ch** or **sh**, we add **es** in the third person singular:

I watch, you watch, he, she, or it watches
we watch,   you watch,   they watch

I fish, you fish, he, she, or it fishes
we fish,   you fish,   they fish

**+es**

**Maybe we should throw it back!**

25

# MORE ABOUT VERBS

## TRANSITIVE VERBS

These verbs need an **object** to complete the sentence. For instance, the verb 'find' can't be used without an object:

The detective finds…    This sentence is not complete.

The person doing something is the **subject** of the sentence. If the subject is doing something to someone or something, that becomes the **object** of the sentence. Words like give, find, do, catch, make and ask should all have an object.

The detective finds **a clue**.
The man can do **nothing**.
The girl gives **a present**.
She made **it** herself.

## INTRANSITIVE VERBS

An **intransitive verb** doesn't need an object. Speak, lie, listen, sit, die, and rise are all verbs of this kind.

The class listens.
The dog sits.

POLICE TRAINING SCHOOL

## ACTIVE OR PASSIVE

Verbs can be used actively or passively. **Active** verbs are used when the subject of the sentence is doing the action.

Carmel speaks Spanish.
Martin feeds the dog.

**Passive** verbs are used when the subject of the sentence is having something done to him or her.

Carmel is being spoken to.
The dog is being fed.

Si!

It is usually better to use active verbs rather than passive verbs, as they help to make your writing more direct and lively.

27

# TENSES

The verb **tense** shows the time when an action takes place—the past, present or future. (The word tense itself comes from the Latin word *tempus*, meaning time.)

Present tense:
Now I **go** to school.

Past tense:
I **went** to playgroup when I was a toddler.

Future tense:
I **will** go to college when I am older.

There are two ways of changing verbs to show the timing of the action.

Present tense:   I **help**

Past tense:     I **helped**

The other is to use auxiliary verbs such as 'is, are, am' (see page 24) to change the timing:

Present tense:   I **am** helping

Past tense:     I **was** helping

Future:       I **will** help

**HAY!**

**WHAT?**

**Present tense** (taking place now)
Here are some verbs used in the **present tense**:

I **help** at the stables.
You **ask** the question.
He **calls** to his dog.

Why did you call him 'Fetch'?

If something is happening continuously, there is another form of the present tense:

She is sleeping late this morning.
We are walking in the woods.

OK Hansel, which way?

'Sleeping' and 'walking'
are **present participles**. They are
used with auxiliary verbs (is, are)
to show continuous action.

## MORE ABOUT TENSES

**Past tense** (took place before now, has already happened). These verbs are used in the **simple past tense**:

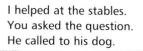

> I helped at the stables.
> You asked the question.
> He called to his dog.

Other forms of the past tense use auxiliary verbs with a **past participle** which is usually the same as the past tense. To form the past tense in regular verbs, add **ed** or just **d** in verbs such as 'save' which end in e. Here are examples of auxiliary verbs being used to create the past tense:

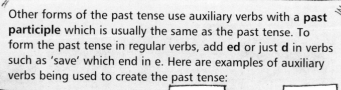

> I have helped
> I had helped

**+ed**    **+d**

**Warning** There are however many verbs where both the past tense and the past participle are irregular – *see opposite*.

**Future tense** (will take place)
Unlike some other languages, English has no future form of the verb itself. To show the **future tense**, you have to use auxiliary verbs, as in these examples:

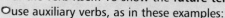

> I **will help** at the stables.
> You **will ask** the question.
> He **will call** his dog.

## Conditional tense

There is one more tense you need to know – the **conditional tense**. This says that an action is **conditional** on something else – that is, it may take place if something else happens first.

I **would help** at the stables if I could have a horse.
You **would ask** the question if you dared.
He **would call** to his dog if he had not lost his voice.

## IRREGULAR VERBS

Although the **present participle** in all verbs ends in **ing**, the **past participle** can change considerably in irregular verbs, causing problems. An auxiliary verb such as have or had is always needed before the past participle. Look at these:

*I'm rather tense at present.*

| Present tense | Past tense | Past participle |
|---|---|---|
| I am | I was | I have been |
| I begin | I began | I have begun |
| I break | I broke | I have broken |
| I catch | I caught | I have caught |
| I drink | I drank | I have drunk |
| I eat | I ate | I have eaten |
| I fly | I flew | I have flown |
| I forget | I forgot | I have forgotten |
| I get | I got | I have got |
| I go | I went | I have gone |
| I hear | I heard | I have heard |
| I know | I knew | I have known |
| I ride | I rode | I have ridden |
| I ring | I rang | I have rung |
| I run | I ran | I have run |
| I sing | I sang | I have sung |
| I swim | I swam | I have swum |
| I tear | I tore | I have torn |
| I write | I wrote | I have written |

31

## ADVERBS

An **adverb** can be used either to add to or qualify the meaning of a word (a verb or adjective) or to alter that meaning slightly.

There are four main groups of adverbs, which tell how, when, where or how much something happens. 'How' adverbs are mostly formed from adjectives by adding **ly**. Here are some examples:

| | |
|---|---|
| soft | softly |
| brilliant | brilliantly |
| proud | proudly |
| magnificent | magnificently |
| high | highly |

Sometimes when an adjective is changed into an **adverb**, the spelling also has to change:

| | |
|---|---|
| easy | easily |
| greedy | greedily |
| happy | happily |

But instead of ending in **ly**, adverbs sometimes look exactly like adjectives:

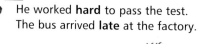

He worked **hard** to pass the test.
The bus arrived **late** at the factory.

**'When' adverbs** show when something happens. Here are a few:

> now   yesterday   soon   immediately   today
> before   since   seldom   often   already

They had **already** found the treasure.

**'Where' adverbs** show where something happens. Here are some examples:

> everywhere   here   outside   nowhere
> above   behind   in   out

They looked **everywhere** for the keys.

**'How much' adverbs** show to what extent something is happening. These are some of them:

> quite   almost   completely   very
> too   hardly   so   less

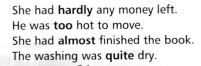

She had **hardly** any money left.
He was **too** hot to move.
She had **almost** finished the book.
The washing was **quite** dry.

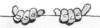

## MORE ABOUT ADVERBS

The main or **simple** form of an adverb is the one found in a dictionary:

clearly    quickly    near    soon

**Comparative adverbs** compare two things or people:

Tim ran quickly but Chris ran **more quickly**.
My birthday will be soon but yours is **sooner**.

Lucky!

**Superlative adverbs** compare three or more people or things:

Tim and Chris ran quickly,
but Sarah ran **most quickly**.

I've only got little legs.

May I please have the soonest of the appointments available?

Short adverbs usually add **er** to form a comparative adverb, and **est** to form a superlative one.

| Simple | Comparative | Superlative |
|--------|-------------|-------------|
| near | nearer | nearest |
| soon | sooner | soonest |

Longer adverbs become the comparative by adding **more**, and the superlative by adding **most**:

| Simple | Comparative | Superlative |
|--------|-------------|-------------|
| happily | more happily | most happily |

carefully     more carefully     most carefully

**EXCEPTIONS**

| Simple | Comparative | Superlative |
|--------|-------------|-------------|
| badly (or ill) | worse | worst |
| far | farther | farthest |
| little | less | least |
| much (or many) | more | most |
| well | better | best |

Teacher says I'm the best in the class.

And guess who teacher says is the worst?

# CONJUNCTIONS

When you want to join words or groups of words together, you use a **conjunction**. The way it is used can change the meaning of a sentence. The simplest ones are:

> and   but   nor   or   yet   for   so

The brothers argue **but** they are friends.
She was not in the kitchen, **nor** was she in the shed.
Gillian **and** her sister are in Canada.

Conjunctions can come before a reason:
because   since   as

The family is going to the cinema
   **because** it's her birthday.

They can also be used to show time:

> when   whenever   before   after
> until (or till)   as   while   since

Wash that fruit **before** you eat it.
I haven't seen you **since** we had lunch last week.

Sometimes a conjunction can be two words:

> either/or   neither/nor   both/and   so/as   whether/or

Please be **so** good **as** to help me.
We're going for a picnic **whether** it rains **or** shines.
**Either** you give me that money back,
   **or** I will tell my father.

Some conjunctions are used to show contrasting views or opinions. These are:

whether/or   while   as   although   though   even if

I'm going out **even if** it rains.

It's too wet to go out!

# PREPOSITIONS

A **preposition** is put in front of a noun or pronoun to show where, when or how the noun or pronoun is connected with another word in the sentence. Prepositions often show position or location. Here are some examples:

>The ladder leans **against** the wall.
>I can stay **until** five o'clock.
>The path runs **alongside** the stream.

Prepositions are mostly short words such as:

>to  at  on  in  up  down  with  of  for
>between  towards  over  by  across  near
>under  through  off  upon  among
>along (and alongside)  under (and underneath)
>into  beneath  since  until  beside  within
>beyond  about  after

>They sailed the boat **on** the pond.
>The ball went **over** the hedge.
>He drove the car **between** two stone pillars.

Some prepositions are made up of groups of words:

>as far as  on top of  in spite of
>except for  by means of  away from
>out of  due to  because of

>The kitten was **on top of** the fridge.
>He won the race **in spite of** his sore leg.
>The bird flew **out of** the nest.

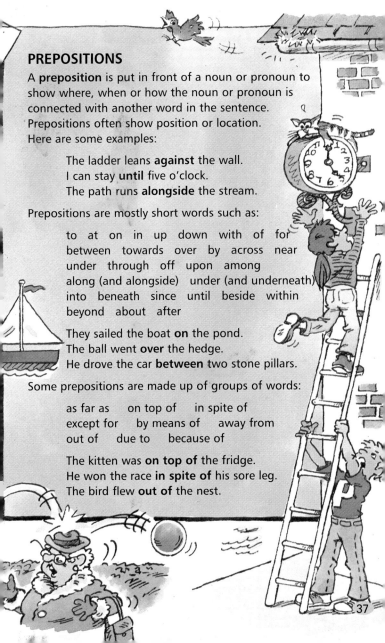

## PUNCTUATION

Full stops (.), commas (,), and question marks (?) are all part of **punctuation**, which helps to make sense of written English.

Here is a passage with no punctuation at all.

> have you ever seen a starfish last summer when I was at the seaside I found a deep rock pool in it were two crabs and a starfish the starfish which was bright orange clung to the rocks

The same passage is much easier and clearer to read when it is punctuated.

> Have you ever seen a starfish? Last summer when I was at the seaside I found a deep rock pool. In it were two crabs and a starfish. The starfish, which was bright orange, clung to the rocks.

## LONG STOPS

A **long stop** is used to end a sentence. A full stop (.) – also called a period – a question mark (?) and an exclamation mark (!) are all long stops.

**Full stop**

The punctuation mark we see most often is the full stop, at the end of a statement.

The telephone is ringing.

You will sometimes see a full stop after an abbreviation where the last letters are missing, such as v. for versus announcing a football match, but this usage is now disappearing. In contractions which use the last letter after missing letters – for example Dr for Doctor, full stops should not be used.

STOP!

I know when I'm not wanted.

Don't question me, question Mark!

## Question mark

When we ask someone a question, we show that it is a question by the way we speak. Since we cannot do this in writing, we use a question mark instead. A question is usually followed by an answer.

What time is it?

It is two o'clock.

Sometimes just one word is a question in itself, and this too is followed by a question mark.

Who? What? Why? Where? When? How?

## Exclamation mark

As with a question mark, an exclamation mark acts as a full stop. It is most often used after an interjection, which is a word showing surprise, shock or pleasure:

Brilliant!

Oh! Ah! Ouch! Dear me!

Exclamation marks can also come after sentences or phrases to strengthen a command or to show amusement.

Pay attention!

You don't say!

It is best to use exclamation marks sparingly, so that each one will have a greater impact.

> I'm just having a bit of a breather.

## SHORT STOPS

A **short stop** is used within a sentence to make the sense clearer. Commas (,), hyphens (-), dashes (–), brackets (), colons (:) and semi-colons (;) are all short stops.

### Comma

**Commas** are put in a written sentence to help it to make sense (not, as is sometimes thought, at the place where you would take a breath before reading on).

> Jennie and Rosie put on their best dresses, because they were going to a party.

Commas are also used after names in a list or within a set of instructions.

> Left here, right at the next lights, up to the roundabout and straight on.

### Hyphen

Many compound words (that is, words put together to make one word) have **hyphens** or short dashes in them. Some town names also have hyphens. Here are some examples:

> far-off   Stratford-upon-Avon   Stoke-on-Trent
> left-handed   made-up   Weston-super-Mare

Sometimes hyphens are optional. For example, 'out-of-date' is usually written with hyphens, but the meaning is still clear without them. On the other hand, 'man-eating tiger' needs a hyphen because the meaning changes without it.

**That's what they think!**

### Dash

A **dash** is longer than a hyphen.
Dashes are used before and after a secondary thought or additional information (a **clause**) in a sentence.

> They were out for the evening – without the children – for the first time in years.

You can also use a single dash if you want to add an extra thought at the end of a sentence.

> John remembered his hat and scarf – but he forgot his gloves.

### Bracket

**Brackets** can also be used before and after a secondary thought or extra piece of information. Brackets are always used in pairs, never singly.

> They took a picnic (and some books to read) for their trip to the seaside.

### Colon

**Colons** are used immediately before a list or quotation. This is the only way the colon should be used.

> Three photographs were on show: a wedding group, a baby kicking its legs in the air, and a girl in graduation robes.

### Semi-colon

A **semi-colon**, surprisingly, is seen more often than a colon. It is used to join two related sentences and can be used instead of conjunctions such as 'and' and 'but'.

The building had to be pulled down; it was unsafe.

41

## INVERTED COMMAS

**Inverted commas** (" "/' ') are upside-down commas used at the beginning and end of written speech. Sometimes there are two " ", and sometimes there is only one ' '. They can also be called quotation marks or speech marks.

'Where is he?'
"Here she is!"
'There they are.'
"Let's go out."

The whole of a spoken sentence goes inside the quotation marks, including the full stop, question mark or exclamation mark at the end.

Sometimes a spoken sentence is split in two, and then inverted commas must be put round each part of the sentence. Take care with commas when using quotation marks – they are needed to separate the words spoken from the rest.

"I don't think," she said slowly, "they meant any harm."

Note that the second half of the sentence does not begin with a capital letter.

When speech is reported in newspapers or TV news broadcasts, no inverted commas are required, since the actual words are not used.

The police officer said, "We see no reason to suspect foul play."

**Reported speech** – The police said they saw no reason to suspect foul play.

WHO STOLE
Henrietta?
starring
Miss Smith's class

But this is a case of 'fowl play'.

And you've cooked your goose as well, Jeeves.

Exhibit A

**Fun punctuation**    :–)    happy

People who write to one another on computers via the worldwide Internet have invented some new punctuation of their own. These marks are called 'smileys', and you read them sideways on:

:–(    sad
;–)    wink

My son is starring in Shakespeare's 'Omelette'.

THE BUTLER DID IT.

43

## APOSTROPHE

IS — ISN'T
DOES — DOESN'T
HAS — HASN'T
DID — DIDN'T
CAN — CAN'T

If you see an **apostrophe** (') in a word, it can mean one of two things.

Sometimes words are shortened when speaking or in written speech (but are usually in full in textbooks or formal letters). In this case, an apostrophe takes the place of a letter or letters that have been left out. For example, **isn't** means "is not", with the apostrophe where the letter **o** has been left out. Others are:

| | | | | |
|---|---|---|---|---|
| I've | = I have | hasn't | = has not. |
| who'd | = who would | haven't | = have not |
| it's | = it is | doesn't | = does not |
| there's | = there is | can't | = can not |
| who've | = who have | who's | = who has |
| I'll | = I will | she's | = she is |
| you're | = you are | | |

An apostrophe can also mean that something belongs to someone – Damien's bike is the bike belonging to Damien. (This is called the **possessive case**.)

IT'S MY BIKE!

You're so possessive.

Here are some rules to help you with belonging words.

**1** When there is only one owner (that is, the word is singular), use the apostrophe followed by **s**.

a man**'s** life (the life of a man)
Jane**'s** trainers (the trainers belonging to Jane)
Ben**'s** schoolbag (the schoolbag belonging to Ben)
a bird**'s** nest (the nest of a bird)

RIP
A BODIE
1901-1997

44

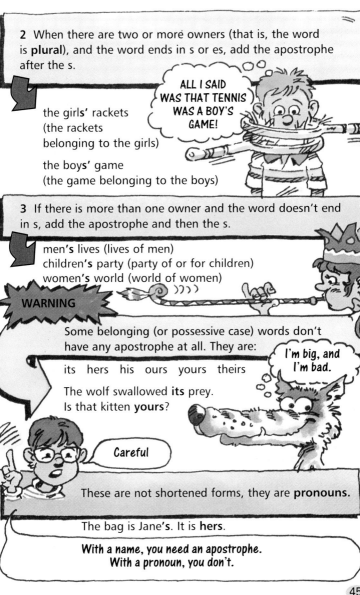

**2** When there are two or more owners (that is, the word is **plural**), and the word ends in s or es, add the apostrophe after the s.

ALL I SAID WAS THAT TENNIS WAS A BOY'S GAME!

the girls' rackets
(the rackets belonging to the girls)

the boys' game
(the game belonging to the boys)

**3** If there is more than one owner and the word doesn't end in s, add the apostrophe and then the s.

men's lives (lives of men)
children's party (party of or for children)
women's world (world of women)

**WARNING**

Some belonging (or possessive case) words don't have any apostrophe at all. They are:

I'm big, and I'm bad.

its   hers   his   ours   yours   theirs

The wolf swallowed **its** prey.
Is that kitten **yours**?

Careful

These are not shortened forms, they are **pronouns**.

The bag is Jane**'s**. It is **hers**.

With a name, you need an apostrophe.
With a pronoun, you don't.

## SPELLING – AND ITS RULES

To speak good English, you need grammar. To **write** good English, you need grammar, punctuation and spelling.

About five centuries ago, people spelt words much as they liked. Even printers were known to spell the same word in several different ways on the same page in a book!

GUD MURNEN TO YUW SYMEN.

GOWD DEY YUNG JOSIF.

Between then and now, dictionaries came into being, and written English was tidied up. Spelling was standardised, although English has more irregular spellings than many other languages. But there are several rules to help you to spell correctly.

### I BEFORE E

The most famous spelling rule in the whole of the English language is 'i before e except after c'. The problem with this one is that it only works when ie and ei sound like a long ee, as in field.

**i before e**

| | |
|---|---|
| piece | achieve |
| relief | yield |
| brief | field |
| believe | retrieve |
| frieze | niece |

**but after c**
conceive
conceit
receive
receipt

And even then there are exceptions:

seize   weird   species   weir

Sometimes ei sounds like i:

height   neither   either   sleight

Or it can sound like ai:

rein   neighbour   skein   reign
eighty   weigh   deign   feign

When ie and ei sound like e as in egg, you'll just have to learn the words!

friend   leisure

Finally, a really nasty one:

lieu (it means instead of, and sounds like loo)

Even really good spellers have to use the dictionary for these.

## SILENT LETTERS

Over half the alphabet can appear as silent letters in words. From the sound of the word, no one would know those letters were there at all. And they can be found at the beginning, the middle or the end of words.

**a**    treadle   bread

**b**    lamb   tomb   aplomb   dumb   undoubtedly
      limb   bomb   comb

**c**    scissors   science   scintillate   scene   scent

**d**    edge   bridge   ledge   fridge   fudge
      hedge   trudge   badge   dredger   dodge

**e**    appears at the end of many words –
      *see* page 56

| h | honour   honest   heiress   hour   school schooner   scheme |
|---|---|
| k | knight   knapsack   knave   know   knock   knew knee   knowledge   knit   knuckle   knead   knife |
| l | would   talk   folk   yolk   psalm alms   should (but think about shoulder, where the l is heard!) |
| n | hymn   autumn   column |
| p | pneumatic   pneumonia psalm   receipt   psychic psychiatry   pseudonym psychology |
| s | isle   island   aisle |
| t | listen   rustle   wrestle   whistle   castle   gristle |
| u | guarantee   biscuit   guardian   guess   guest guide   guild   guitar   guinea pig |
| w | write   wrong   wretched   wrist wrap   wreck   wrestle   wriggle   wreath playwright   wrinkle   overwrought |

Listen

Sssh!

49

# STRANGE COMBINATIONS

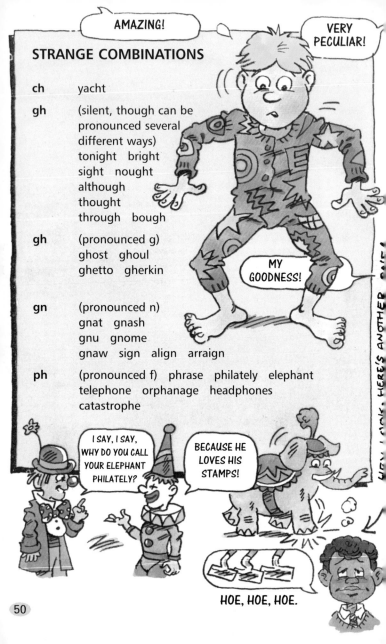

**ch**  yacht

**gh**  (silent, though can be pronounced several different ways)
tonight  bright
sight  nought
although
thought
through  bough

**gh**  (pronounced g)
ghost  ghoul
ghetto  gherkin

**gn**  (pronounced n)
gnat  gnash
gnu  gnome
gnaw  sign  align  arraign

**ph**  (pronounced f)  phrase  philately  elephant
telephone  orphanage  headphones
catastrophe

AMAZING!

VERY PECULIAR!

MY GOODNESS!

HEY LOOK, HERE'S ANOTHER ONE!

I SAY, I SAY, WHY DO YOU CALL YOUR ELEPHANT PHILATELY?

BECAUSE HE LOVES HIS STAMPS!

HOE, HOE, HOE.

## HOMOPHONES

**Homophones** are words which sound exactly the same but have different meaning and spelling.

There are a surprising number of these. Here are just a few:

bare/bear  bean/been  border/boarder
bough/bow  coarse/course  dew/due
fair/fare  flew/flue  heard/herd
hour/our  hymn/him  knew/new
meat/meet  pear/pair/pare  plane/plain
queue/cue  sail/sale  serial/cereal
so/sow/sew  waist/waste

### Some other confusing words

| noun | verb |
|------|------|
| some advice | to advise |
| a practice | to practise |
| a licence | to license |

In these, the noun is always spelt with a c. The verb is always spelt with an s. Alphabetical order will help you to remember – noun and c come before verb and s.

## PREFIXES

The meanings of many words are changed by adding letters to the beginning (called a **prefix** – pre means before), or at the end (called a **suffix** – suf means after).

Now you're my ex-boyfriend!

### Prefixes

Here are some of the main ones:

| | |
|---|---|
| anti (against, opposite) | anticlockwise |
| bi (two) | bilingual |
| circum (around) | circumnavigate |
| com (with) | committee |
| contra (against) | contradiction |
| em (in) | empower |
| ex (out of) | expel |
| inter (between) | interview |
| mis (wrong) | mistake |
| pro (for) | protagonist |
| re (back, again) | recognise |
| tri (three) | triangle |
| un (not) | unacceptable |

YOU ARE THE PROTAGONIST AND I AM EMPOWERED TO EXPEL YOU.

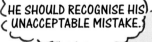

HE SHOULD RECOGNISE HIS UNACCEPTABLE MISTAKE.

I am incapable of defrosting.

Some prefixes give the main word its opposite meaning:

| de | defrost devalue decompose |
| dis | dislike dishonest disapprove |
| in | inattention incapable inconvenient |
| un | unkind unlock untidy |

I DISLIKE YOUR DISHONESTY AND DISAPPROVE OF THE MANNER IN WHICH YOU HAVE DEVALUED THAT T-SHIRT.

WELL, EXCUSE ME!

HELLO, I'M RICH INTELLIGENT AND HANDSOME

**An English oddity**

| combustible | means will catch fire |
| incombustible | means won't catch fire |

BUT flammable and inflammable BOTH mean will catch fire.

# SUFFIXES

The amusement was most admirable

Your kindness is most attractive.

Some suffixes turn the main word from a verb into a noun:

| | |
|---|---|
| exist | existence |
| amuse | amusement |

ADMIRABLE

ATTRACTIVE

Others turn verbs into adjectives:

| | |
|---|---|
| admire | admirable |
| attract | attractive |

Special suffixes are used as verb endings to modify the meaning.

| | |
|---|---|
| ed | burned |
| ing | cheating |
| ise | standardise |

CHEATING!

SSH, SOFTLY.

Lastly, adverbs are formed by adding ly:

clearly    softly

+ly

WHAT DID YOU SAY?

## Spelling changes

Adding a suffix to a word often means that the spelling changes. Here are some rules to help you with this. When your main word ends with a consonant, and the suffix you want to add begins with a consonant, simply add the ending without any change:

A treat!

treat + ment = treatment

## Doubling the consonant

For most words with a short vowel sound, ending with a single consonant, double that consonant when adding a suffix, such as ing, that starts with a vowel.

mop/ping    big/gest    hot/ter    rag/ged

I feel ill.

If the word you want to add to ends in l after a vowel, double the l before adding **er**, **ed** or **ing**:

level/led    carol/ling    travel/ler

Exceptions to this rule are words that end in r, x, w or y:

tear/ing    blow/ing    box/er
know/ing    say/ing    draw/ing

If your main word has two consonants at the end, or more than one vowel, **don't** double the consonant:

rain/ing    (two vowels – a, i)
keep/er    (two vowels – e, e)
break/ing    (two vowels – e, a)
hang/er    (two consonants – n, g)

If you've worked out the spelling and you're still not sure – look it up in your dictionary. There are some awkward exceptions that lots of people get wrong, such as targeted and riveted.

55

## WORD ENDINGS

MMPH!

### Silent e

In English, many words include silent letters – that is, letters that are not sounded when the word is said. **Silent e** is one of the most frequent of these.

When a word ends with a silent e and you want to add a suffix that begins with a **consonant** (ment, ful, less, ly), you don't need to change your main word:

Restaurant

force + ful = forceful
time + less = timeless
sincere + ly = sincerely
manage + ment = management

He's a really forceful person!

When the main word ends with a silent e, but your suffix begins with a **vowel** (or a y), drop the e before adding the suffix:

fame/famous   stone/stony   believable/believably
nerve/nervous   criticise/criticism

EEEE!

Some exceptions: mileage, agreeable.

### Words ending in ce and ge

With words that end in **ce** or **ge**, where you need a suffix starting with a or o, leave the e in:

    manage + able    = manageable
    notice + able    = noticeable
    courage + ous    = courageous

There are however exceptions to this as well, such as prestigious (from prestige), so – use your dictionary if you're not sure.

### Words ending in ie

When you want to add **ing** to verbs ending in ie, drop the e and change the i to a y:

    vie/vying    tie/tying    lie/lying

No one is lazier than you! Get on with your work!

### Words ending in y after a consonant

Change the y to an i before adding suffixes such as **ed**, **es**, **er**, **eth**, **ly**, **ness**, **ful** and **ous**:

    eighty + eth     = eightieth
    duty + es        = duties
    lazy + ness      = laziness
    lazy + er        = lazier
    mystery + ous    = mysterious
    beauty + ful     = beautiful
    multiply + ed    = multiplied
    busy + ly        = busily

### Words ending in y after a vowel

Keep the y when adding suffixes such as **er**, **ing** or **ed**.

    destroy    destroying    destroyed
    pray       praying       prayer
    buy        buying        buyer
    prey       preying       preyed

+er?

57

# SYNONYMS AND ANTONYMS

## Synonyms

When you are looking for a different word to say the same thing, you need a **synonym**. Here are some suggestions to start you off:

rapid/speedy/quick
happiness/joy/euphoria
old person/senior citizen/veteran
plan/design/organise
disaster/calamity/catastrophe
amusing/entertaining/diverting
thoughtful/pensive/meditative
thorough/meticulous/diligent
accuse/blame/charge
leave/resign/quit
weak/feeble/enervated

Your thesaurus and your dictionary will both help you to find the right word or phrase.

## Antonyms

Words with opposite meanings are called **antonyms**.

happy/sad
cool/warm
hot/cold
dull/bright
sweet/sour
rough/smooth
interesting/boring
cheerful/depressed
transparent/opaque
noisy/silent
strong/weak

*Speech bubbles:*
HO HO!
I'm enervated.
I'm a veteran.
I'm pensive.
I'm very diverting.
I was only being cheerful and now I'm depressed.
**Stop being noisy and stay silent!**
That's interesting.
Boring!

# FIGURES OF SPEECH

When you want to make your writing more powerful or more poetic, you can use a **figure of speech**. You are probably already using some of these without realising it.

A **simile** compares one thing to another, because of some imagined likeness. It does not say that the two things are the same, but that they are alike in some way. A simile uses 'like' or 'as'.

> She smiled **like a cat who'd eaten the cream**.
> He ran **as if his feet had wings**.

A **metaphor** calls one thing by the name of another because of some imagined likeness:

> There were roses in her cheeks – is a metaphor.
> (If you said, her cheeks were like roses, this would be a simile.)

A **rhetorical question** is a question that does not require an answer, because only one answer appears possible:

> Who does not love his country?

**Alliteration** is when sentences or lines of poetry have two or more words starting with the same sound:

> Sing a song of sixpence – is alliterative.

**Euphemism** is using a mild vague expression instead of a strong definite one.

> He has passed away – is a euphemism for 'he died'.

**Onomatopoeia** is using words that sound like what they mean. In:

> A bee was buzzing – the word 'buzzing' is onomatopoeic.

An **epigram** is a short witty saying:

> With friends like you who needs enemies?

She has cheeks like roses.

With friends like you who needs enemies?

59

# WRITE A LETTER!

## Now you can write – write a letter!

There are all sorts of letters. Some are informal, to people you know well – to your best friend who has left the district, or to your mum when you are away on holiday.

Others are slightly more formal – thanking an aunt for the birthday present she sent you, or your hostess for having you to stay on holiday.

And some are very formal indeed, to people you don't know, requesting information or making a complaint. Or you could be thanking someone for an invitation to a party.

First you put your own address at the right-hand side of the page at the top, complete with postcode. You can put commas after each line if you wish, but nowadays such punctuation marks can be left out, since computer users do not put them in. Put the date underneath the address.

Start your letter at the left-hand side, a little way below the date.

Now think about what you want to say, and organise your thoughts into paragraphs. When you have written a number of sentences about a particular thing, and you want to start on something new, you begin a new **paragraph**. You leave a bigger space than usual to show that it's a new subject, and you can indent if you want to, starting the first line of the new paragraph a little way in from the beginning of the previous line.

If you start your letter Dear Sir/Madam, you should end it Yours faithfully

If you know the name of the person you are writing to, end your letter Yours sincerely, and sign it. (Or Best Wishes, or Love from, for people you know better.)

14 Arnfield Road,
Townville,
Westshire W14 5PS

29th September 1997

The Manager,
Sports and Shoes Ltd,
High Street,
Townville.

Dear Sir or Madam,
I bought a pair of trainers from your shop a month ago. I planned to wear them when I went on holiday.

However, only two weeks after I bought them, the sole split open. As a result, sand sea and salt water got inside, and I had to buy a new pair.

I enclose my receipt, and I would like you to refund the cost.

Yours faithfully
Alan Customer
Alan Customer

## SPORTS & SHOES LTD

3 October 1997

A Customer
14 Arnfield Road
Townville
W14 5PS

Dear Mr Customer

Thank you for your letter of September 29 about the pair of trainers that you purchased from us in August.

We are sorry to learn that you had a problem, and we enclose our credit note for £25, which you may exchange for goods or cash, whichever you prefer.

We apologise for the trouble you have been caused.

Yours sincerely

Harold G Baxter

The reply is typed on a word processor. The layout is different for reasons of speed and computer memory.

# WATCH OUT FOR THESE!

Words people often get wrong –
in books, newspapers, signs,
posters and even television:

Watch out!

accessible  accidentally  accommodation
admittance  ancillary  auxiliary  commission
committee  competitive  gauge  guarantee
irresistible  licensed  maintenance
necessary/unnecessary  prejudice

## Grammatical errors

Left is right!

These phrases often cause problems.
The first version is the correct one.

between you and me (not I)
people like you and me (not I)
theirs (belonging to them)/there's (there is)
different from (not than)
protest against (not at)
either this or that
neither this nor that
fewer than five people (number)
less than five pounds (amount)
elder of two children/eldest of three children
bigger of the two/biggest of the three

theirselves does not exist:
the word is themselves

none of these is cheap:
none is singular, therefore
needs a singular verb